# FAITH HUNTER

Author of *Spiritually Fly: Wisdom, Meditations and Yoga to Elevate Your Soul*

Written by Faith Hunter
Designed by Faith Hunter
Printed in the United States of America
www.faithhunter.com

# the return to you

A 52-Week Journal Infused with Mindful
Reflections and Self-Love Affirmations

# contents

Flowing through healing water,
I find solace and a space for
personal reflection.

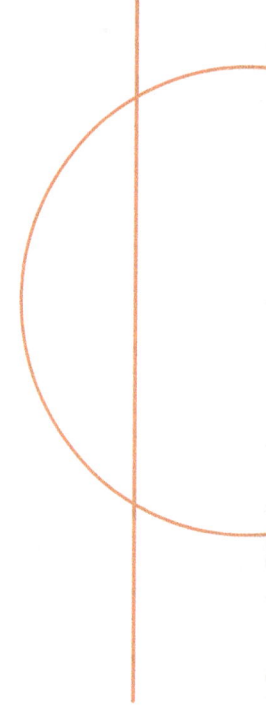

CHAPTER 1

# the return to you

INTRODUCTION

# the return
## to you

A 52-Week Journal Infused with Mindful Reflections and Self-Love Affirmations

In the symphony of life, each of us navigates a path filled with intricate melodies – some harmonious, others dissonant. My journey, like many, has been a tapestry woven with threads of joyous highs, profound losses, heart-wrenching breaks, and transformative rebirths. This reflective book is born from my experiences of navigating life's challenges and the significant shift I moved through at the end of 2022 that resulted in me returning to my home state, Louisiana.

Through each painful parting and every moment of loss over the years, I found solace and strength in the practices that have become the pillars of my life – journaling, meditation, yoga, reflection, and affirmations. These practices, deeply ingrained in my personal and spiritual journey, are the essence of what I've shared in my previous work, "Spiritually Fly." They have been my compass, guiding me back to my highest divine self, even in the darkest of times.

As I embarked on another life shift in Dec 2022, I realized the transformative power of returning to one's essence – a journey back to the core of our being, where our highest, most loving, and vibrantly alive self resides. This journal captures the essence of those realizations and experiences over the past 12 months. It is a guide, a companion, and a reflection of the journey back to one's true self.

The path to returning to our highest selves is not linear; it meanders through the valleys of introspection, climbs the mountains of self-discovery, and sails the seas of emotional depths. Inside these pages, you will embark on a year-long journey divided into four transformative parts: Personal Growth and Self-Discovery, Emotional Wellness and Resilience, Mindfulness and Spiritual Growth, and Positivity and Empowerment. Each section is designed to guide you through the layers of self-reflection, emotional healing, and empowerment.

Personal Growth and Self-Discovery are about peeling back the layers, uncovering the truths about who we are, and embracing the full spectrum of our being. It's about learning to love and accept ourselves with all our complexities and contradictions.

In Emotional Wellness and Resilience, we delve into the heart, learning to navigate our emotions with grace and courage. This section is about building the resilience to face life's challenges and emerge stronger and more emotionally intelligent.

Mindfulness and Spiritual Growth leads us on an inward journey to a place of peace, clarity, and spiritual connection. My hope is that you will find solace in the present moment, embrace the journey of spiritual exploration, and connect deeply with your inner wisdom.

Positivity and Empowerment are about harnessing the power of a positive mindset and stepping into our power. It's rooted in choosing to see the light, even in darkness, and empowering ourselves to live with purpose, joy, and strength.

This journal is more than just a collection of words; it's a personal transformation toolkit. As you journey through these pages, you will find affirmations to uplift your spirit, journal prompts to explore the depths of your soul, and reflections to guide you back to your highest self.

As I share this journey with you, I do so with the vulnerability and openness that has guided my path. The teachings and practices within these pages are those I have used to navigate my life changes – over the years and throughout 2023. They are the practices that have brought me back to a place of love, peace, and empowerment.

As you pause, breathe, and reflect, I invite you to return to your highest, most loving self. It's a journey of healing, transformation, and rejuvenation – a return to the essence of who you are.

Love,

Within the shadows of my discomfort, I uncover the untold stories of my ancestors.

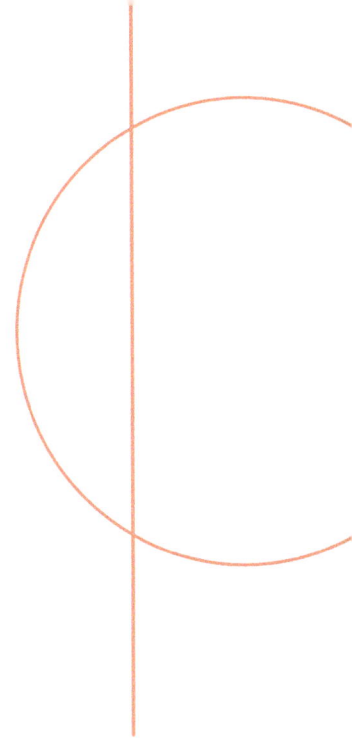

CHAPTER 2

# how to use the journal

NAVIGATING YOUR PATH

# how to use
## the journal

- **Start where you are:** This journey has no perfect starting point. Begin with Week 1, or where you feel most called, based on a section that resonates with your current life.

- **Engage with the affirmations:** Each set of affirmations is a tool for mindset shift and self-empowerment. Read them aloud or silently. Reflect on what they stir in your heart, and let them resonate throughout your week.

- **Dive deep with journal prompts:** The journal prompts are your opportunity for introspection. They are not just questions but gateways to your inner world. Write your responses honestly, allowing yourself to fully explore your thoughts and emotions.

- **Create a routine:** Dedicate a specific time each week for this. Find a rhythm that works for you, whether it's early morning, a quiet evening, or a peaceful weekend moment.

- **Embrace your journey:** This journal is about your unique path. Your responses, emotions, and insights are yours alone. There's no right or wrong way to engage with these prompts – only your way.

- **Seek solitude:** Find a quiet space to be with your thoughts. Select a cozy corner of your home, a peaceful outdoor setting, or any place that feels sacred. Sit within an environment that supports introspection and reflection.

- **Reflect and revisit:** Allow yourself to reflect on your responses. You may find your perspectives shift over time. Feel free to revisit sections or prompts that have a significant impact.

- **Be gentle with yourself:** Transformation is a process that can bring comfort and discomfort. Be gentle with yourself as you navigate through these changes. Give yourself grace and space to grow.

- **Implement insights into your life:** Take the insights from this journal and find ways to integrate them into your daily life. The true power of this journey lies in applying these lessons beyond the pages.

- **Share your journey:** If you feel comfortable, share your journey with trusted friends, family members, or your therapist. Sometimes, saying things out loud gives them more power and allows for shared wisdom and support.

This journal is a reflection of my walk through life's ups and downs, and it's now a part of your journey. Use it as a guide, a source of inspiration, and a reminder of your resilience, power, and capacity for love.

free yourself from the
restrictions of fear
expand into the greatness of
your beauty
dance fiercely in the rivers of
divinity
listen to your intuition and be
guided by your heart

Just as water cleanses and renews, the love and strength from those who came before me wash over my soul, grounding my spirit.

# personal growth and self-discovery

WEEKS 1-13

# personal growth and self-discovery

In the whirlwind of life, where we are often caught in the crossfires of external expectations and internal pressures, the journey of personal growth and self-discovery stands as a beacon of light. It's a journey that beckons us to delve deeper into the essence of who we truly are beneath the layers of societal roles and personal narratives.

Personal growth is not a destination; it's a continuous process of evolving, learning, and expanding. It's about embracing every experience as a valuable lesson that contributes to understanding ourselves and the world around us. When we are in the waters of personal growth, we step out of our comfort zones to question, explore, and challenge the status quo. In these moments of brave exploration, we uncover the most profound truths about ourselves.

Self-discovery, on the other hand, is an intimate and personal journey. It's about peeling back the layers of our identity and understanding our desires, fears, strengths, and vulnerabilities. It's a path of recognizing and celebrating our uniqueness and individuality. Self-discovery is not about finding ourselves, instead, it is about creating ourselves and shaping our identity with intention and purpose.

As a global wellness expert, my life's work has been about guiding others on this path of personal growth and self-discovery. Through breathwork, yoga, meditation, and mindful living, I've witnessed the transformative power of self-awareness. It's a journey that is both challenging and rewarding, filled with moments of introspection, realization, and enlightenment.

The series of affirmations and journal prompts I've crafted are more than just words or exercises; they are tools to aid you on this journey. These affirmations are designed to reinforce positive thinking, instill a sense of self-worth, and encourage a mindset of growth and resilience. Each affirmation is a reminder to embrace your journey, acknowledge your worth, and celebrate your unique path.

The journal prompts, meanwhile, serve as a gateway to deeper reflection. They are invitations to introspect, question, and explore the depths of your being. Journaling is a powerful practice that not only aids in self-expression but also self-discovery. It allows you to articulate your thoughts, emotions, and experiences, providing clarity and insight.

As you move through the affirmations and journal prompts, you are embarking on a journey of self-exploration. You are uncovering layers of your personality, understanding your core values, and aligning with your true purpose. These affirmations and prompts encompass a range of themes – from embracing self-worth and cultivating inner peace to discovering self-identity and nurturing hope. Each theme is carefully chosen to resonate with different aspects of personal growth and self-discovery.

Keep in mind that the road is not always easy. It requires courage to face our truths, strength to embrace our vulnerabilities, and wisdom to learn from our experiences. But the rewards are immeasurable.

As you engage with these affirmations and journal prompts, you'll grow in confidence, clarity, and self-awareness. You'll discover the inner power you never knew and face fears with newfound resilience. You'll learn to navigate life with a deeper understanding of yourself and a greater appreciation for your journey.

This section is about shedding the layers that no longer serve you and embracing your authentic self. As you move through, know that you are not alone. You are part of a community of souls on a similar path, each seeking to uncover their true essence and live their most authentic life.

# WEEK 1

## EMBRACING SELF-WORTH

Let's start powerfully and affirm the beauty of our unique existence. Remember, your worth isn't defined by external validation but by the light you carry within. Embrace your unique qualities and strengths, for they make you irreplaceably special. In every step and every decision, let's honor the truth that we are worthy of love and respect, just as we are. Let's commit to seeing and celebrating our true selves, independent of the world's opinions.

*I am worthy of love.*
*My self-worth is independent of others' opinions.*
*I embrace my unique qualities and strengths.*

## JOURNAL PROMPTS

Reflect on a moment when you felt truly valued for who you are. How can you cultivate more of those moments?

What unique qualities do you possess that make you special and worthy of love?

_____

_____

_____

_____

_____

_____

# WEEK 2

## CULTIVATING INNER PEACE

This week is about rediscovering our sanctuary of inner peace. Recognize that true serenity comes from within and is not shaken by the chaos outside. Let's practice releasing what we cannot control and embrace the calmness that resides in us. Each breath is an opportunity to return to our natural state of peace. Let's journey through our days with the quiet assurance that calmness is always within our reach.

*Inner peace is my natural state, and I return to it easily.*
*I release things out of my control and find serenity.*
*Calmness flows through me in every situation.*

## JOURNAL PROMPTS

Identify a recent situation where you maintained inner peace despite external chaos. How did you achieve it?

What practices or thoughts can you adopt to cultivate a greater sense of calm in your daily life?

_____

_____

_____

_____

_____

_____

# WEEK 3

## NURTURING SELF-COMPASSION

Drop into the gentle embrace of self-compassion. It's about treating ourselves with the same kindness and understanding we generously offer others. Let's recognize that every misstep is not a setback, but a pivotal step in our growth journey. As we move through this week, let's pledge to be our own best friend, speaking to ourselves with love and patience, and nurturing our spirit with the compassion it deserves.

*I treat myself with kindness and understanding.*
*Every misstep is a step in my journey of growth.*
*I give myself the compassion I give to others.*

## JOURNAL PROMPTS

Reflect on a recent misstep and write a compassionate response to yourself about it.

How can you practice more self-compassion in your daily life?

_____

_____

_____

_____

_____

_____

# WEEK 4

## EMBRACING POSITIVITY

This week, let's commit to the power of positivity. It's about choosing to see the light, even when heaviness looms. Remember, our thoughts shape our reality, and by fostering a positive mindset, we attract similar energy. Let's consciously radiate positivity, knowing that it not only uplifts us but also those around us. Each moment is an opportunity to turn towards the radiance within, and let its warmth guide our path.

*I choose positivity in every situation.*
*Positive thoughts and attitudes lead my way.*
*I radiate positivity and attract the same in return.*

## JOURNAL PROMPTS

Think of a time when a positive mindset transformed a challenging situation for you.

How can you cultivate a habit of choosing positivity each day, even in small ways?

_____

_____

_____

_____

_____

_____

# WEEK 5

## CULTIVATING PATIENCE

In a world that constantly rushes us, let's find the strength to pause, breathe, and wait. This week is about honoring the virtue of patience. Patience isn't just waiting; it's maintaining a calm spirit while we wait. It's a quiet strength that brings wisdom and peace. Let's approach our days with the understanding that some of the best things in life unfold in their own time.

*I embrace patience as a path to wisdom and peace.*
*Patience allows me to accept things as they unfold.*
*In patience, I find inner stability and clarity.*

## JOURNAL PROMPTS

Reflect on a situation where patience led to a better outcome.

How can you practice patience in daily activities with yourself and others?

_____

_____

_____

_____

_____

_____

_____

# WEEK 6

## FOSTERING SELF-RESPECT

Self-respect is about recognizing our worth and treating ourselves with the dignity we deserve. Let's honor our boundaries, understanding that they are a vital expression of self-respect. Each decision and each action we take should be guided by a deep respect for ourselves. As we journey through this week, let's remember that respecting ourselves is the foundation for receiving respect from others.

*I treat myself with respect and honor my boundaries.*
*Self-respect guides my actions and decisions.*
*I am worthy of respect from myself and others.*

## JOURNAL PROMPTS

Reflect on how you can better honor your boundaries in personal and professional relationships.

Consider a recent situation where you stood up for yourself. How did it make you feel?

---

---

---

---

---

---

# WEEK 7

## DISCOVERING SELF-IDENTITY

For Week 7, let's delve into the beautiful journey of self-discovery. Each of us is a unique tapestry woven from our experiences, beliefs, and talents. Embracing this diversity within ourselves is not just empowering; it's a celebration of our authenticity. Let's honor our evolving identities, and recognize that each step and realization brings us closer to understanding our truest selves.

*I am on a journey to discover and embrace my true self.*
*My identity is a unique blend of my talents, beliefs, and experiences.*
*I am proud of my evolving identity and journey.*

## JOURNAL PROMPTS

Reflect on aspects of your identity that make you proud. How do they shape your daily life?

Consider a talent or belief you've recently discovered about yourself. How has this contributed to your sense of identity?

_____

_____

_____

_____

_____

_____

# WEEK 8

## NURTURING HOPE

This week is about kindling the flame of hope within us. In times of uncertainty or challenge, it is our connection to hope that whispers, "You will be okay!" Let this divine force light our paths, and provide inner knowing and resilience. When we hold the hand of hope, we open ourselves to possibilities and invite joy and optimism into our hearts. Let's cherish and nurture the wellspring of hope, and allow it to guide us through life's journey.

*Hope lights my path and guides me through challenges.*
*I hold onto hope in all circumstances.*
*Hope is a wellspring of strength within me.*

## JOURNAL PROMPTS

Recall a time when hope helped you overcome a difficult situation.

What are some ways you can nurture hope in your daily life, especially during challenging times?

_____

_____

_____

_____

_____

_____

# WEEK 9

## CELEBRATING MIND AND BODY CONNECTION

The harmonious balance between mind and body is a dance of wellness where each influences the other, creating a symphony of health and personal alignment. Celebrating this unity is not just about physical health; it's about recognizing how our thoughts, emotions, and physical sensations are interconnected. Let's engage in practices that honor this connection, finding our true power in the unity of our being.

*My mind and body are in perfect harmony.*
*I celebrate the unity of my physical and mental well-being.*
*In mind-body, I find my true power.*

## JOURNAL PROMPTS

Identify activities that help you feel a deeper connection between your mind and body.

How can you incorporate consistent practices into your routine that enhance this mind-body connection?

_____

_____

_____

_____

_____

_____

# WEEK 10

## EMBRACING LIFE'S JOURNEY

Each twist and turn, and every high and low, is a chapter in our story filled with invaluable lessons. Let's approach our paths with gratitude, knowing that every experience contributes to our evolution. As we navigate the week, let's cherish each moment as a precious part of our ongoing adventure.

*I embrace every twist and turn of my life's journey.*
*Life is filled with invaluable lessons and joys.*
*I am grateful for my unique journey and its destinations.*

## JOURNAL PROMPTS

Think of a significant twist or turn in your life's journey. What did it teach you?

How does embracing the unpredictability of life enrich your personal journey?

_____

_____

_____

_____

_____

_____

# WEEK 11

## CULTIVATING INNER WISDOM

The profound wisdom that dwells within each of us must be honored. Our life experiences, both the triumphs and trials, have cultivated a deep wisdom that we carry. It's a guiding light, helping us navigate through the complexities of life. Trusting this wisdom means trusting ourselves, our intuition, and our past learnings. Let's make decisions with the confidence that our inner wisdom will always lead us along a path of growth.

*I trust the wisdom that resides within me.*
*Each experience in my life enriches my inner wisdom.*
*My inner wisdom guides my decisions.*

## JOURNAL PROMPTS

Think of a decision you made recently that was guided by your inner wisdom. What as the result and how did it feel?

How can you create space in your daily life to listen more to your inner wisdom?

_____

_____

_____

_____

_____

_____

# WEEK 12

## EMBRACING SELF-GROWTH

This week is about recognizing that each day and each experience is a step towards becoming the best versions of ourselves. Embracing growth is embracing change – a journey filled with learning, challenges, and magnificent triumphs. Let's commit to our growth in giant leaps and the small everyday choices that shape our path. No matter how small, each step is movement and self-evolution.

*I am committed to my personal growth and evolution.*
*Every step I take is part of my growth journey.*
*I embrace the process of becoming the best version of myself.*

## JOURNAL PROMPTS

Identify a personal growth goal you are currently working toward. What steps are you taking to achieve it?

How do you measure your growth and progress? Reflect on the changes you've seen in yourself.

_____

_____

_____

_____

_____

_____

# WEEK 13

## CULTIVATING MINDFUL AWARENESS

This week, let's focus on cultivating mindful awareness. It's about being fully present in each moment and embracing life as it unfolds. Mindful awareness isn't just a practice; it's a way of living that brings clarity and peace. Take the opportunity to slow down, breathe, and truly engage with the present. As we move through our days, let's observe each moment, knowing that in awareness lies the beauty of life.

*I cultivate mindful awareness in my daily life.*
*Each moment is an opportunity to be fully present and aware.*
*Mindful awareness brings clarity and peace to my life.*

## JOURNAL PROMPTS

What are some moments where you can be more mindfully present in your daily life?

Reflect on a recent experience where being mindfully aware changed your perspective.

_____

_____

_____

_____

_____

_____

the resilience of my ancestors is
embedded in my DNA
the depth of my breath fortifies my soul
aligned with divine awareness my heart
stays true
armed with love I'm ready for the
unexpected

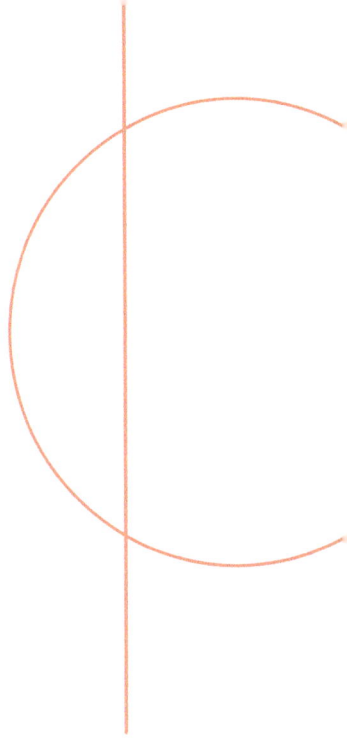

CHAPTER 4

# emotional wellness and resilience

WEEKS 14-26

# emotional wellness and resilience

Emotional wellness and resilience are like twin beacons guiding us through the ebbs and flows of our experiences. They are not mere concepts but living, breathing aspects of our existence that color every moment, every decision, and every interaction. I've come to understand that the foundation of a fulfilling life lies in nurturing our emotional well-being and cultivating the resilience to face life's myriad challenges.

Emotional wellness encompasses understanding, accepting, and managing our feelings with compassion and bravery. It's not about avoiding or suppressing emotions, but about navigating them with grace and intelligence. When we are emotionally well, we are better equipped to handle stress, connect with others, and make decisions that align with our deepest values. It's a state of being that allows us to experience life fully, with all its complexities and beauty.

Resilience is the strength that helps us bounce back from adversity. It's our ability to adapt to change, to rise from setbacks, and to emerge stronger and wiser. Resilience doesn't mean we don't feel pain or face difficulties; rather, it means we have the capacity to move through experiences and grow from them.

Although our lives are deep personal journeys filled with unique moments, there are common threads that bind us. These moments are about building a relationship with our emotions, understanding our triggers, and developing wellness strategies that work for us. It's also about nurturing connections with others, which can become powerful relationships and serve as sources of support and growth.

This series of affirmations and prompts reminds us of our strength, adaptability, and emotional intelligence. As they provide space for reflection and exploration, and they encourage the deepening of your emotional landscape, understanding your reactions, and envisioning new ways of being. They also invite you to celebrate your successes, learn from life's lessons, and find balance and joy in everyday living. So definitely soak up those special moments to pause, listen to your intuition, and trust your ability to navigate life's complexities.

As you engage in self-discovery, the themes we explore – from fostering self-trust and emotional intelligence to embracing adaptability and celebrating individual achievements – are all facets of emotional wellness and resilience. Each week, as you reflect on these themes, you are building a stronger, more resilient self.

Remember, this healing work is not a destination but an ongoing process. It requires patience, effort, and, most importantly, a compassionate approach towards oneself. Let these affirmations and journal prompts be your allies in this journey. Let them guide you, challenge you, and inspire you. Embrace them as tools to explore the depths of your emotional world, build resilience, and live a life of emotional wellness.

# WEEK 14

## FOSTERING SELF-BELIEF

Let's nurture the seeds of self-belief within us. Believe in your infinite potential and the power of your dreams. Each step forward, fueled by belief in our abilities, paves the path to success. Remember, self-belief isn't just about achieving goals; it's about embracing the journey, knowing that you are capable, worthy, and deserving of every triumph that comes your way.

*I believe in my abilities and potential.*
*My dreams are achievable and within my reach.*
*Self-belief is the foundation of my success.*

## JOURNAL PROMPTS

Reflect on a time when your self-belief led you to achieve something significant.

How can you strengthen your belief in yourself when facing doubts or challenges?

_____

_____

_____

_____

_____

_____

# WEEK 15

## ENHANCING SELF-LOVE

This week is dedicated to deepening self-love. Let's embrace ourselves wholly, acknowledging our strengths and embracing our flaws. Self-love is the foundation from which positivity flourishes. As we radiate love and acceptance from within, we attract the same warmth and affection from the world. Let's be a beacon of love, not just towards ourselves but also radiating it outwards.

*I deeply and completely love and accept myself.*
*Self-love radiates from me and attracts positivity.*
*I am a magnet for love in all its forms.*

## JOURNAL PROMPTS

What are five things you love about yourself and why?

How does practicing self-love change the way you interact with others and the world?

_____

_____

_____

_____

_____

_____

# WEEK 16

## FOSTERING COMPASSION

It's time to journey through the heartwarming path of compassion. In showing compassion, not only towards others but also towards ourselves, we build bridges of understanding and kindness. Let's remember that every act of compassion, no matter how small, has the power to transform lives. As we practice compassion, we enrich our personal growth and deepen our connections with those around us.

*I practice compassion towards myself and others.*
*Compassion enriches my relationships and personal growth.*
*Through compassion, I connect deeply with the world around me.*

## JOURNAL PROMPTS

Recall a recent instance where you showed compassion. How did it impact both you and the other person?

What are some ways you can practice self-compassion in moments of self-criticism or doubt?

_____

_____

_____

_____

_____

_____

# WEEK 17

## BUILDING CONFIDENCE

Let's step into the empowering light of confidence. It's about trusting our abilities, making decisions with conviction, and facing life's challenges head-on. Remember, confidence isn't just a feeling; it's an action. It's taking those bold steps, even when we feel uncertain. With each step, our confidence grows, building a stronger foundation for future success.

*I am confident in my abilities and decisions.*
*Confidence empowers me to take bold steps forward.*
*Each successful experience boosts my confidence.*

## JOURNAL PROMPTS

Reflect on a recent situation where your confidence led to a positive outcome. What can you learn from this?

How can you build and maintain your confidence in areas where you feel uncertain?

_____

_____

_____

_____

_____

_____

# WEEK 18

## PROMOTING INNER HARMONY

Inner harmony is finding that delicate balance where our thoughts, emotions, and actions align peacefully. It's not just about tranquility; it's about understanding and accepting the complexities within us. Let's embrace this week with a heart that seeks balance and a spirit that radiates peace.

*I live in harmony with myself and the world around me.*
*Inner peace and harmony are my guiding principles.*
*I balance my life with tranquility and harmony.*

## JOURNAL PROMPTS

Identify areas in your life where you seek greater harmony. What steps can you take towards achieving this?

Reflect on how inner peace contributes to a sense of harmony in your life.

_____

_____

_____

_____

_____

_____

# WEEK 19

## ENHANCING MINDFULNESS

This week is about deepening our practice of mindfulness. Let's embrace the beauty of being fully present, experiencing each moment in its fullness. Mindfulness is more than a practice; it's a way of living that brings richness to our experiences and depth to our connections. Let's journey through this week with a mindful heart, savoring each moment with awareness and gratitude.

*I am fully present in every moment.*
*Mindfulness enriches my experiences and connections.*
*I embrace each moment with awareness and gratitude.*

## JOURNAL PROMPTS

What are some daily activities where you can practice being more mindful?

Reflect on a recent experience where being mindful changed your perspective or reaction.

_____

_____

_____

_____

_____

# WEEK 20

## PRIORITIZING HEALTH AND WELL-BEING

Time to direct our focus on the holistic nurturing of our health and well-being. Remember, each healthy choice is an act of self-love and a step towards transforming our lives for the better. Let's honor our bodies and minds as vessels and sacred temples deserving of our utmost care and attention. Embrace this week as an opportunity to cherish and nurture the gift of health.

*My health is a precious gift that I nurture and cherish.*
*Every healthy choice positively transforms my life.*
*I honor my body and mind through loving care and attention.*

## JOURNAL PROMPTS

Reflect on how making healthy choices has positively impacted your life.

What new health and well-being practices can you incorporate into your routine?

_____

_____

_____

_____

_____

_____

# WEEK 21

## ACKNOWLEDGING PERSONAL POWER

Personal power is about recognizing the strength and confidence within us to create the life we desire. Our inner power is a force of intention and purpose, guiding us through life's journey. Let's use this power not just to navigate our paths but to pave new ones, creating positive change in our lives and in the world around us.

*I possess the power to create positive change in my life.*
*My personal power is a source of strength and confidence.*
*I use my inner power to live my life with purpose and intention.*

## JOURNAL PROMPTS

Identify a situation where you can use your personal power to create positive change.

How does acknowledging your personal power affect your self-perception and actions?

_____

_____

_____

_____

_____

# WEEK 22

## CELEBRATING SUCCESS

Let's turn our focus towards celebrating success. Every achievement, whether big or small, is a milestone in our journey and deserves recognition. Remember, success is not just a destination; it's a journey filled with learning, growth, and joy. Let's savor each step, celebrating our triumphs with a heart full of gratitude and joy.

*Every achievement, big or small, is a cause for celebration.*
*I acknowledge and celebrate my successes with joy.*
*Success is a journey, and I savor every step.*

## JOURNAL PROMPTS

Reflect on a recent success, big or small, and how it made you feel.

How can you better acknowledge and celebrate your successes in life?

_____

_____

_____

_____

_____

_____

# WEEK 23

## ENCOURAGING RESILIENCE

We should honor our ability to bounce back from adversity that shapes our strength and character. Each challenge we face is an opportunity for our resilience to grow, teaching us that we are stronger than we ever imagined. Let's approach every hurdle with the knowledge that it's not just about enduring but growing through the process.

*I am resilient in the face of adversity.*
*Resilience guides me through life's ups and downs.*
*I face my challenges with bravery, and my resilience grows.*

## JOURNAL PROMPTS

Think of a time when your resilience helped you overcome a difficult situation.

How can you cultivate resilience in your daily life to better handle challenges?

---------------------------------------------

---------------------------------------------

---------------------------------------------

---------------------------------------------

---------------------------------------------

---------------------------------------------

# WEEK 24

## CULTIVATING SELF-TRUST

Self-trust is about listening to our intuition and believing in our judgment. It is the cornerstone of every decision we make and every step we take. As we journey through this week, let's remind ourselves that trusting our abilities and instincts is the first step to living a fulfilling and authentic life.

*I trust my intuition and judgment.*
*Self-trust guides me to make wise decisions.*
*Believing in myself builds a strong foundation of trust.*

## JOURNAL PROMPTS

Reflect on a decision where trusting your intuition led to a positive outcome.

How can you strengthen your sense of self-trust in everyday situations?

_____

_____

_____

_____

_____

_____

# WEEK 25

## EXPANDING MINDFULNESS

Let's deepen our connection with the present through mindfulness. It's about expanding our awareness and opening ourselves to the richness of each moment. Mindfulness is not just a practice; it's a way of being that allows us to fully engage with life, bringing a deeper understanding and appreciation for the world around us.

*I expand my awareness through mindfulness.*
*Mindfulness connects me deeply with the present moment.*
*Through mindfulness, I gain a deeper understanding of life.*

## JOURNAL PROMPTS

Identify a daily activity where you can practice expanding your mindfulness.

Reflect on how mindfulness has impacted your understanding of a recent event or situation.

_____

_____

_____

_____

_____

_____

# WEEK 26

## HONORING AUTHENTICITY

Together, let's embrace the power of authenticity. It's about being true to ourselves in every aspect of life. Authenticity isn't just an expression; it's a way of living that attracts genuine connections and opportunities. Let's honor our true selves and find strength in our authenticity, knowing that it's our most natural and powerful state of being.

*I honor who I am in all aspects of life.*
*Being authentic is the truest expression of myself.*
*My authenticity attracts genuine connections and opportunities.*

## JOURNAL PROMPTS

What does being authentic mean to you, and how do you express it in your daily life?

Think of a time when being authentic led to a positive outcome in your life.

---

---

---

---

---

---

there's no running, hiding, or deflecting
be brave
see the self
kiss the harsh edges of the self
fall down and cry in the self
make waves to unnerve the self
crawl in the darkness of the self
rumble in the cave with the self
when the walls fall down
breathe into the fullness of the self

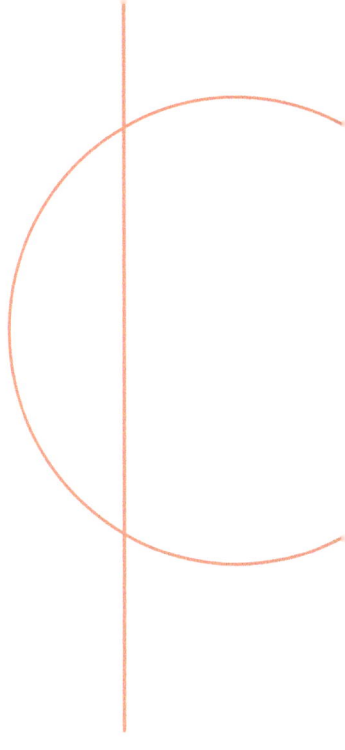

CHAPTER 5

# mindfulness and spiritual growth

WEEKS 27-39

# mindfulness and spiritual growth

Mindfulness and spiritual growth are integral threads that add depth, color, and meaning to our existence. Since connecting with the earth while gardening with my grandmother, I have always believed in the transformative power of mindfulness and the profound journey of spiritual growth. These are not just practices, but ways of living that deeply enrich our life experience.

Mindfulness is about being present in the moment, fully engaging with life as it unfolds. It's a practice of awareness where we observe our thoughts, feelings, and sensations without judgment. In a world that often feels chaotic and overwhelming, mindfulness is a sanctuary of peace and clarity. It allows us to experience life more fully, savor each moment, and connect with ourselves and others in a more meaningful way.

Spiritual growth, on the other hand, is a journey of the soul. It's about exploring our deepest beliefs, connecting with a higher purpose, and understanding our place in the universe. This journey is deeply personal and unique to each individual, yet it unites us in our quest for meaning, understanding, and connection.

In my work and personal life, I have seen firsthand how mindfulness and spiritual growth can transform us from within. Practices rooted in mindfulness and spiritual growth have the capacity to heal, inspire, and open our hearts to a world of possibilities. They teach us to be resilient in the face of adversity, find joy in the simplest things, and live with peace and purpose.

I've crafted this collection of affirmations and journal prompts to engage you on a soulful journey. Each affirmation is a sweet drop of wisdom, a grounded reminder to be present, and an opening on your spiritual path. I hope they will guide you through the complexities of life with a mindful and spiritual perspective.

The journal prompts complement the affirmations by offering a space for soul-stirring reflection and exploration. They invite you to walk a mindful path, uncover insights, and connect with your inner wisdom. As you drop in, this set allows you to articulate your thoughts and feelings and see your spiritual path more clearly.

The themes we explore – from nurturing inner joy and embracing stillness to cultivating gratitude and finding peace – are the many layers of mindfulness and spiritual growth. Each one offers a unique perspective and an opportunity for deep personal development.

I invite you to breathe and be present in each moment, to connect deeper with your spiritual self, and to embrace life with an open heart and mind. My soul encourages you to explore your beliefs, find joy in the journey, and grow in ways you never thought possible. Embrace them as tools for living more mindfully and growing spiritually; in them lies the key to a more fulfilling and meaningful life.

# WEEK 27

## NURTURING INNER JOY

This week, let's embrace nurturing our inner joy. It's about recognizing that joy is a choice and a strength that resides within us, independent of our circumstances. Focusing on what brings us joy allows us to transform our perspective and approach life with a renewed sense of purpose and happiness. Let's make a conscious effort to connect with and cultivate our inner joy, making it a guiding light in our lives.

*I nurture inner joy as a source of strength and resilience.*
*Joy is within me, regardless of external circumstances.*
*I choose to focus on what brings me joy.*

## JOURNAL PROMPTS

What are some simple activities or moments that bring you inner joy? How can you incorporate more of these into your daily life?

Reflect on how maintaining a focus on joy influences your mood and perspective, even in challenging times.

---------------------------------

---------------------------------

---------------------------------

---------------------------------

---------------------------------

# WEEK 28

## STRENGTHENING EMOTIONAL RESILIENCE

Strengthening our emotional resilience is rooted in embracing life's challenges with grace and understanding, knowing that each experience helps us grow stronger. Emotional resilience doesn't mean we don't feel the weight of our emotions; it means we navigate them with wisdom and fortitude. Let's commit to nurturing our emotional resilience and turning challenges into opportunities for growth.

*I am emotionally resilient and handle life's ups and downs with grace.*
*My emotional resilience grows stronger each day*
*I navigate my emotions with understanding and strength.*

## JOURNAL PROMPTS

Think of a recent challenge you faced. How did you demonstrate emotional resilience, and what did you learn from the experience?

What daily practices can you adopt to strengthen your emotional resilience?

_____

_____

_____

_____

_____

# WEEK 29

## HONORING AUTHENTICITY

Honoring our authenticity is about being true to ourselves in every aspect of our lives, and understanding that our authenticity is our greatest gift. In a world that often pressures us to conform, let's celebrate our uniqueness and the genuine connections it brings. Let's remind ourselves that being authentic is the truest and most fulfilling expression of who we are.

*I honor my authenticity in all aspects of life.*
*Being authentic is the truest expression of myself.*
*My authenticity attracts genuine connections and opportunities.*

## JOURNAL PROMPTS

Reflect on what authenticity means to you and how you express it in your life.

Think of a time when being authentic led to a positive experience or opportunity.

_____

_____

_____

_____

_____

_____

# WEEK 30

## EMBRACING MINDFUL LIVING

Let's dedicate this week to the active practice of mindful living. It's about fully experiencing each moment, and finding clarity and peace in our daily lives. By embracing the present with awareness, we open ourselves to a deeper understanding of our surroundings and inner selves. Let's cherish each moment, understanding that mindfulness enriches our lives in profound ways.

*I live each moment with mindfulness and presence.*
*Mindful living brings clarity and peace to my day.*
*I embrace the present moment with full awareness.*

## JOURNAL PROMPTS

What are some specific moments in your day when you can practice being more mindful?

Reflect on the impact that mindful living has on your daily interactions and self-awareness.

_____

_____

_____

_____

_____

_____

# WEEK 31

## DEEPENING SPIRITUAL YOUR PRACTICE

Deepening our spiritual practice is centered on committing to a journey that enhances our understanding of the world and brings joy and enlightenment. Our spirituality is a personal path of discovery and growth that we nurture daily. Let's embrace this journey with an open heart, cherishing each step as we grow and evolve spiritually.

*My spiritual practice deepens my understanding of myself and the world.*
*Every day, I commit to my spiritual growth.*
*Spirituality is a journey that brings joy and enlightenment.*

## JOURNAL PROMPTS

Identify one aspect of your spiritual practice you would like to deepen or explore further.

How does your spiritual practice contribute to your sense of joy and enlightenment?

_____

_____

_____

_____

_____

_____

# WEEK 32

## CULTIVATING SELF-COMPASSION

This week, let's cultivate the art of self-compassion. It's about treating ourselves with the same kindness and understanding we offer others. Self-compassion is a daily practice, especially in moments of struggle or self-doubt. Let's gently remind ourselves that we deserve compassion and kindness, which is vital to our overall well-being and growth.

*I treat myself with kindness and compassion.*
*Self-compassion is a gift I give myself every day.*
*In moments of struggle, I remember to be compassionate towards myself.*

## JOURNAL PROMPTS

Reflect on how practicing self-compassion can change your response to challenging situations.

What are some ways you can remind yourself to practice self-compassion daily?

_____

_____

_____

_____

_____

# WEEK 33

## FINDING PEACE IN SOLITUDE

Let's embrace the peace that comes with solitude. This week is a time for massive deep self-reflection and connection with our inner selves. Solitude isn't loneliness; it's a cherished space where we rejuvenate our spirit and find clarity. Let's value and enjoy our moments alone, recognizing them as opportunities for personal growth and inner peace.

*Solitude brings me peace and self-reflection.*
*In moments of solitude, I connect deeply with my inner self.*
*I value and enjoy my time alone, as it rejuvenates my spirit.*

## JOURNAL PROMPTS

Reflect on how solitude impacts your sense of peace and self-awareness.

What activities or practices in solitude help you reconnect with yourself?

_____

_____

_____

_____

_____

_____

# WEEK 34

## CELEBRATING MINDFUL MOMENTS

Each small instance of mindfulness is a celebration of life, a reminder to cherish the present. It's about finding joy in the ordinary and understanding that mindfulness in even the smallest things can bring great happiness. Let's commit to recognizing and appreciating these moments, allowing them to enrich our daily lives.

*I find joy in mindful moments throughout my day.*
*Each mindful moment is a celebration of being alive.*
*Mindfulness in small things brings great joy.*

## JOURNAL PROMPTS

Identify a daily routine activity where you can practice mindfulness to find joy.

Reflect on how these mindful moments impact your overall sense of well-being.

_____

_____

_____

_____

_____

_____

# WEEK 35

## EXPLORING SPIRITUAL INSIGHTS

Our spiritual journeys are filled with wisdom and lessons that guide us toward understanding and peace. Let's approach our spiritual practice with openness, ready to receive the insights that help illuminate our path. As we explore these insights, we deepen our connection with ourselves and the world around us.

*My spiritual journey offers valuable insights into my life.*
*I am open to the wisdom and lessons of my spiritual path.*
*Spiritual insights guide me toward greater understanding*
*and peace.*

## JOURNAL PROMPTS

Reflect on a recent insight or lesson gained from your spiritual journey.

How can you be more open and receptive to spiritual insights in your daily life?

_____

_____

_____

_____

_____

_____

# WEEK 36

## PRACTICING MINDFUL COMMUNICATION

Mindful communication involves engaging in conversations with full awareness and empathy, genuinely listening, and connecting with others. It is more than just exchanging words; it's about building more robust, and meaningful relationships. Let's strive to be fully present in our conversations, fostering understanding and connection.

*I communicate mindfully, with awareness and empathy.*
*Mindful communication strengthens my relationships.*
*In every conversation, I strive to be fully present and understanding.*

## JOURNAL PROMPTS

Think of a recent conversation where mindful communication could have improved the outcome.

What steps can you take to practice more mindful communication in your interactions?

_____

_____

_____

_____

_____

_____

# WEEK 37

## EMBRACING STILLNESS

In moments of quiet and calm, we find true peace and renewal. Stillness is not just a lack of movement; it's a sacred space for reflection, growth, and deep connection with our inner selves. Let's seek and cherish these moments of stillness, allowing them to rejuvenate our spirit and bring clarity to our minds.

*In stillness, I find peace and renewal.*
*I embrace moments of stillness for reflection and growth.*
*Stillness is a sacred space where I connect with my inner self.*

## JOURNAL PROMPTS

Identify moments in your day when you can practice embracing stillness.

Reflect on how stillness contributes to your sense of peace and self-connection.

_____

_____

_____

_____

_____

_____

# WEEK 38

## FINDING CLARITY THROUGH MINDFULNESS

Let's focus on the clarity that mindfulness brings. It's about using mindfulness to clear the fog in our minds, and to see our path and decisions more clearly. As we practice mindfulness, we gain a deeper understanding of ourselves and our lives, helping us navigate with greater awareness and insight. Let's cherish the clarity of being fully present in each moment.

*Mindfulness brings clarity and understanding to my life.*
*In moments of mindfulness, I see my path more clearly.*
*I embrace mindfulness as a tool for clarity in my thoughts*
*and decisions.*

## JOURNAL PROMPTS

Reflect on an instance where practicing mindfulness clarified a situation or decision.

How can you incorporate mindfulness into your daily routine to maintain clarity in your life?

_____

_____

_____

_____

_____

_____

# WEEK 39

## EXPLORING INNER WISDOM

Inner wisdom is about trusting our inner compass, allowing it to guide us toward deeper truths and understanding. In the quiet moments of reflection, we can connect more deeply with this wisdom. Let's embrace the insights and guidance it offers, trusting that it will lead us on the right path.

*I trust and explore the inner wisdom that guides me.*
*My inner wisdom is a compass that leads me to truth and understanding.*
*In moments of quiet, I connect deeply with my inner wisdom.*

## JOURNAL PROMPTS

Reflect on a decision where your inner wisdom guided you to the right choice. How did this feel?

What practices can you incorporate to better connect with and trust your inner wisdom?

_____

_____

_____

_____

_____

_____

living fully in my purpose
walking faithfully along my path
trusting my heart as the guide

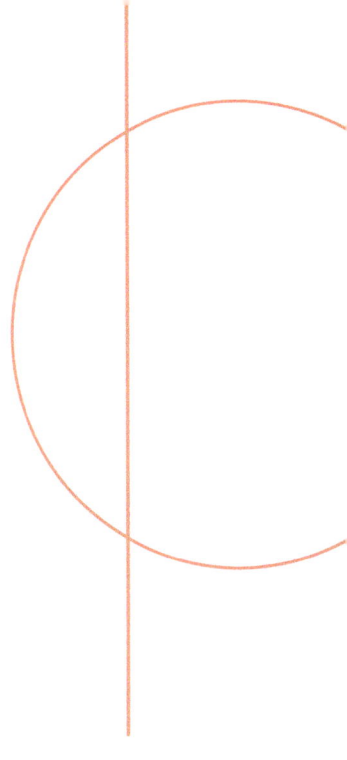

CHAPTER 6

# positivity and empowerment

# positivity and empowerment

The inner pursuit of positivity and the embrace of personal empowerment are key to unlocking our fullest potential. Maintaining a positive outlook and empowering ourselves through mindful practices are not just fleeting states of mind but profound tools that can reshape our lives.

Positivity goes beyond seeing the glass as half full; it's about creating a mindset that actively seeks out and focuses on the good in ourselves, others, and our situations. It's a way of viewing life that enhances our resilience, fuels our happiness, and propels us forward. By choosing positivity, we improve our well-being and impact those around us, creating a ripple effect of optimism and hope.

Empowerment is recognizing and embracing our divine magic, uniqueness, and mind-blowing potential. It's about taking charge of our lives, making conscious decisions, and acting in ways that align with our deepest values, goals, and highest good. Empowerment is the inner strength that enables us to face life's unexpected moments with courage, determination, and faith.

I have dedicated myself to helping others discover and nurture these aspects within themselves. But this dedication is beautifully inspired by my inner work and a journey that requires and continues to require a commitment to my body, mind, and soul. Through positivity and empowerment, we can overcome obstacles, achieve our goals, and lead lives filled with purpose, joy, and inner peace. These affirmations and journal prompts are potent statements, grand beacons of positivity, and a declaration of self-empowerment. They are designed to uplift your spirit, reinforce your power, and remind you of your inherent worth.

The introspective journal prompts provide a space for deeper exploration and refined reflection. They are opportunities to challenge limiting beliefs and help you envision limitless new possibilities. As you engage with this set, you will embark on a transformative expedition of fostering compassion, building confidence, embracing adaptability, and acknowledging self-worth. Each week, as you reflect, you reinforce your steps towards a more empowered and positive life.

Along waves of magnifying your daily life, I invite you to embrace this practice with a positive mindset, to recognize and utilize your strengths, and to take actions that resonate with your authentic self. This collection encourages you to navigate life's ups and downs with grace, and to view the lessons as opportunities for growth and empowerment.

Let collection be your trusty companion as you amplify your subconscious and elevate your soul. Let them inspire you, challenge you, and empower you. Embrace them as inner flames for cultivating a positive outlook and stepping into your HIGHEST power as you taste the immense rewards of living unapologetically as yourself.

# WEEK 40

## THE HEART'S EMBRACE

This week invites us to walk the nurturing path of compassion with even more sweetness. As we extend our hearts towards ourselves and others, we're reminded of the shared human experience that binds us. Each gesture of compassion is a thread in the tapestry of our collective humanity. By cultivating compassion, we not only foster personal growth but also sow seeds of empathy and connection in the world around us.

*With every breath, I weave the fabric of compassion into my being.*
*The tender roots of compassion nurture my growth.*
*Compassion is the melody that harmonizes my connection with the universe.*

## JOURNAL PROMPTS

Recall a moment of compassion that you've recently extended or received. How did this exchange of kindness affect you both emotionally?

Explore moments where you've been hard on yourself. How can you offer the same compassion to yourself that you would give to a dear friend?

_____

_____

_____

_____

# WEEK 41

## THE ESSENCE OF SELF-LOVE

Let's dive deeper into the sacred waters of self-love. With each breath, let us wrap ourselves in the warmth of complete acceptance, recognizing that our perceived imperfections are facets of our brilliance. From this wellspring of self-love, we draw the strength to infuse our lives and the lives of others with positivity. Let us stand as lighthouses of love, illuminating our paths and guiding others along theirs.

*I am wholeheartedly at peace with who I am.*
*My self-love is a beacon, drawing in boundless positivity.*
*Love in its purest form flows to and from me effortlessly.*

## JOURNAL PROMPTS

Reflect on the unique traits that define your essence. Why do these qualities fill you with love for yourself?

In what ways does nurturing self-love influence your relationships and your perception of the world around you?

_____

_____

_____

_____

_____

# WEEK 42

## CULTIVATING INNER ASSURANCE

Inner assurance is an acknowledgment that confidence is more than a transient state—it is a deeply rooted belief in our own abilities. It's the courage to act, the strength to stand firm in our convictions, and the resilience to face challenges with a steadfast heart. As we journey through this week, let each step taken in confidence be a brick laid on the path to our future achievements.

*In every endeavor, I trust my capabilities with unwavering belief.*
*My inner assurance guides me to stride forward with courage.*
*With every achievement, my wellspring of confidence overflows.*

## JOURNAL PROMPTS

Reflect on a moment when your inner assurance was the key to your success. What insights did it bring about your capabilities?

Contemplate ways in which you can nurture a steady stream of confidence, especially in moments filled with doubt.

_____

_____

_____

_____

_____

_____

# WEEK 43

## CELEBRATING INDIVIDUALITY

Our uniqueness is not just what sets us apart; it's our superpower. Embracing and honoring our differences is an act of self-love and empowerment. Remember that being different is a gift we should cherish every day. In celebrating our individuality, we inspire others to do the same, creating a world rich in diversity and beauty.

*My uniqueness is my superpower.*
*I celebrate my individuality.*
*Being different is a gift I honor every day.*

## JOURNAL PROMPTS

Reflect on what makes you unique and how it has contributed to your life.

How can embracing and celebrating your individuality impact your daily interactions and self-esteem?

_____

_____

_____

_____

_____

_____

# WEEK 44

## HARNESSING THE POWER OF POSITIVITY

Let's wholeheartedly embrace the transformative energy of positivity. It's more than a choice; it's a lifestyle. By nurturing optimistic thoughts and attitudes, we become architects of a vibrant reality. Intentionally emitting this radiant energy, we become beacons of light for ourselves and those we encounter. Each day presents a fresh chance to align with the brightness of our spirits, guiding us on a path of luminosity and hope.

*In every moment, I consciously choose positivity as my guide.*
*I lead my life with a mindset of optimism that paves my path.*
*Positivity flows from me, creating a ripple effect of vibrant energy.*

## JOURNAL PROMPTS

Describe an instance where your optimism was the key to transforming a challenge.

What daily practices can you introduce to foster a spirit of positivity throughout your day?

_____

_____

_____

_____

_____

_____

# WEEK 45

## CULTIVATING PATIENCE WITH GRACE

This week invites us to weave patience into the fabric of our daily lives with grace. In the quiet moments of life's unfolding, let's gently remind ourselves of the calm endurance within us. Patience is not merely waiting; it's the art of compassionate presence with our becoming. It's about greeting each moment with the tender touch of time, knowing that our most beautiful revelations arrive not in a rush, but in a hush.

*I nurture patience as a tender guardian of my peace.*
*I allow life's tapestry to unfold with serene acceptance.*
*Through patience, I gain a clear vision and gentle strength.*

## JOURNAL PROMPTS

Think of a recent moment where patience brought you clarity or peace. How did you cultivate it within yourself?

What daily affirmations or routines can you introduce to foster a space of patience in moments of waiting or transition?

---

---

---

---

---

---

# WEEK 46

## EMBRACING UNAPOLOGETIC RADICAL SELF-CARE

Radical self-care is a vibrant act of self-preservation and a celebration of our worth. It's about boldly placing our well-being at the forefront, not as an afterthought but as a fundamental right. Let's engage in self-care that's as essential as breathing—unapologetically and with full-hearted dedication.

*I embrace radical self-care with unapologetic fervor, honoring my needs.*
*Through self-care, I reclaim my energy and vitality.*
*I dedicate time to my well-being, acknowledging it as my rightful priority.*

## JOURNAL PROMPTS

Design a self-care ritual that feels indulgent and deeply nourishing, and commit to integrating it into your life.

Journal about the transformative effects of steadfast self-care on your mental, physical, and emotional health.

_____

_____

_____

_____

_____

_____

# WEEK 47

## HARMONIZING YOURSELF AND SURROUNDINGS

The art of harmony rests in creating a symphony between our inner world and the environment, a balance that resonates with the quiet wisdom of our soul. Inner harmony transcends mere quietude—it weaves acceptance and understanding into the fabric of our existence. Let's walk through this week with intentions set on balance, and let our spirits emanate the peace we nurture within.

*Each breath I take weaves harmony into my being.*
*I am guided by the serene rhythm of inner peace, aligning my inner world with the outer.*
*Life's dance moves gracefully to my tune of tranquility and balance.*

## JOURNAL PROMPTS

Explore areas of your life where harmony feels distant. Envision practical steps to invite balance into these spaces.

Ponder the role of inner peace in crafting a harmonious existence. How does it shape your daily interactions and overall well-being?

_____

_____

_____

_____

_____

# WEEK 48

## BUILDING EMOTIONAL INTELLIGENCE

Cultivating emotional intelligence is more than understanding our feelings; it's about managing them wisely and empathetically. Emotional intelligence is crucial for enhancing our relationships and deepening our self-awareness. As we navigate our emotions with intelligence, we foster a greater sense of understanding and harmony both within ourselves and in our interactions with others.

*I navigate my emotions with intelligence and understanding.*
*Emotional intelligence enhances my relationships and*
*self-awareness.*
*I am in tune with my emotions.*

## JOURNAL PROMPTS

Reflect on a recent situation where emotional intelligence helped you navigate a challenge.

What steps can you take to further develop your emotional intelligence in daily interactions?

_____

_____

_____

_____

_____

# WEEK 49

## EMBRACING VITALITY

This week is an ode to our holistic health, a commitment to the sacred vessel that carries us through life. Let's recognize every nutritious meal, every restful night, and every mindful moment as acts of reverence for our well-being. Cherishing our health is not merely about prevention or maintenance; it's about celebrating life in its fullest, most vivid form.

*I treasure my well-being as the foundation of a vibrant life.*
*Each choice for health is a choice for life.*
*With gratitude, I treat my body and mind as cherished sanctuaries.*

## JOURNAL PROMPTS

Contemplate the positive shifts that have unfolded from your wellness choices. How have these choices echoed through various aspects of your life?

Envision new wellness practices you can introduce. How can these practices become pillars of your daily life?

_____

_____

_____

_____

_____

# WEEK 50

## EMBRACING YOUR TRUE SELF

We will now celebrate the essence of our true selves. Authenticity goes beyond mere honesty; it's the courageous act of fully being. It's about removing the masks we wear and standing in our truth. As we align our actions with our authentic self, we naturally draw towards us a life filled with authenticity and the richness it brings. Let's walk in our truth this week and watch the world open up in response.

*In every action, I am aligned with my true self.*
*My sincerity is my signature, my authenticity, my art.*
*The universe responds to my genuineness with abundant grace.*

## JOURNAL PROMPTS

Journal about the essence of authenticity for you. How do you bring this authenticity into your daily life?

Recall an instance where your authentic self directly influenced a positive outcome or opened a door of opportunity.

_____

_____

_____

_____

_____

_____

# WEEK 51

## ACKNOWLEDGING SELF-WORTH

YES, it is time to fully acknowledge our self-worth. Remember, our value does not fluctuate based on external circumstances or opinions. It's inherent, constant, and unwavering. Recognizing and honoring this innate worth is essential for our emotional resilience. Let's remind ourselves daily that we deserve respect, kindness, and love simply because we exist.

*My self-worth is inherent and unwavering.*
*I recognize and honor my innate value.*
*I am deserving of respect and kindness always.*

## JOURNAL PROMPTS

Reflect on what self-worth means to you and how you can actively honor it in your life.

Consider a time when you stood up for your worth. How did it impact your feelings of self-worth?

_____

_____

_____

_____

_____

_____

# WEEK 52

## UNLEASH YOUR HIGHEST AND MOST DIVINE SELF

As we culminate our journey, let's boldly step into the arena of our personal power. This is more than recognizing our capabilities; it's about dynamically engaging with the world, wielding our inner strength to forge realities brimming with positivity. With every breath, let's affirm our role as divine beings, changemakers, and forces of nature using our intrinsic power to manifest our aspirations and leave indelible marks of progress on our paths.

*I am the divine architect of my life.*
*My wisdom and power fuel my journey with unwavering confidence.*
*Purposefully, I channel my inner force to sculpt a life rich with intention and action.*

## JOURNAL PROMPTS

Visualize a scenario where your assertive energy becomes the catalyst for uplifting transformation.

Reflect on the profound impact of embracing your power. How does it shape your identity and propel your decisions?

---

---

---

---

---

never underestimate the power of your existence

CHAPTER 7
# final drops of love
EMBRACE OUR HIGHEST SELF

# embrace your
## highest self

As you come to the end of this journal, remember that this is not the end of your journey. This is a beautiful milestone on your continuous path of growth and self-discovery. You have delved into the depths of your heart, explored the contours of your mind, and touched the essence of your spirit.

THOUGHTS TO CARRY WITH YOU:

- *Your Journey is Ongoing:* The path of self-improvement is infinite. Each day offers new opportunities to learn, grow, and evolve. Keep the practices of journaling, meditation, reflection, and affirmations close, as they are golden glitters of light in this journey of life.

- *You Are Your Greatest Teacher:* Trust in the wisdom that resides within you. The insights and revelations you have uncovered in this journal are your guides. Listen to them, honor them, and let them light your way.

- *Embrace All Facets of Your Being:* You're a glorious tapestry of experiences, emotions, and thoughts. Embrace all facets of your being, even those that challenge you. Each part of you is worthy of love and understanding.

- *Carry Your Lessons Forward:* As you move forward, carry the lessons and insights you have gained. Let them inform your decisions, guide your actions, and shape your interactions with the world.

- *Return to This Journal:* Whenever you feel lost, overwhelmed, or in need of guidance, return to this journal as a way of returning to your soul. It will always be here to remind you of your journey, your worth, and to reconnect you with your highest self.

- *Share Your Light:* You have a unique light that the world needs. Share your journey, your insights, and your wisdom with others. Your story can inspire, heal, and empower.

As you close the old chapter of your life, know that you are stepping into the world renewed, rejuvenated, and reconnected with your most divine and loving self. The journey of "The Return to You" is my gift of resilience and love that I hope you continue to use and share.

Navigate the complexities and beauties of life, hold onto the lessons and insights. Know that the words I've shared, and powerful insights you've written are not just words on a page, but living parts of your journey and shaping who you are.

Returning to your highest self is a flowing river of growth and self-discovery. Within the ripples, depths, and shallow waves, continue to be compassionate with yourself, forever mindful of your relationship to your soul, and always willing to embrace change. Each day offers a new opportunity to live more authentically, love more deeply, and shine more brightly.

Finally, as you open the door to your true glow, do so with the knowledge that you have everything you need within you. Your return is a journey home to the heart of who you truly are — a being of love, wisdom, and boundless magic.

May your journey be filled with abundance and always stay Spiritually Fly!

Love,

each morning I rise
offerings are made
gratitude is given
before my feet kiss the earth
honoring spirits with breath
opening my heart's doorway
faith releases into portals
transporting blessings into reality
while renewing trust in her divine presence

realizing my potential
to manifest the life I desire
washing my mind and heart
free of pain and suffering
cultivating the brilliance
to see beauty at my feet
walking a path of service
paved by my ancestors
I rise from the muck
designed by God
to be the lotus
dancing passionately in the light
this is my time to
live out my dharma
to shine where darkness
held me back
to be guided by
love and purpose
infused with fire and strength
this propels me past my
insecurities and fears
into a realm that is magical and bright
it is time for me to be

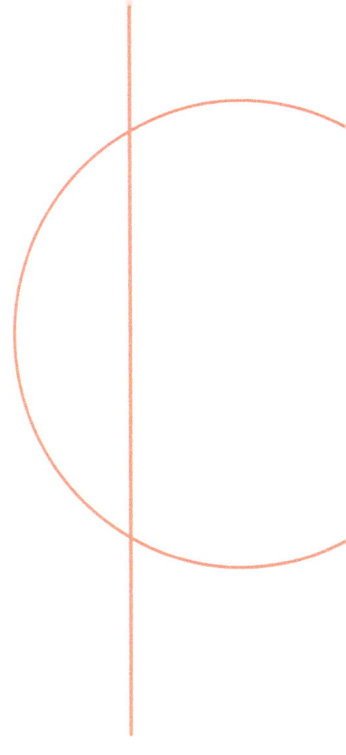

# about the author

FAITH HUNTER

# embrace your
## highest self

Faith Hunter, a globally recognized wellness authority and luminary, embarked on her transformative yoga and meditation journey in the early 1990s. Navigating through the profound emotional landscape of her brother Michael's battle with AIDS, Faith sought solace in mindfulness and introspection, unearthing the profound depths of her soul. Since 2003, she has inspired yogis and wellness seekers worldwide, imbuing her teachings with her personal journey of resilience and healing.

With a foundation in marketing (BS from Grambling State University) and an MBA from Loyola University, Faith blends her business acumen with her spiritual teachings. Formerly the visionary force behind two renowned yoga studios in Washington, DC, Faith has evolved her focus to the digital realm with Elevate by Faith app, an innovative online sanctuary. Elevate by Faith harmoniously blends ancient practices with the nuances of contemporary culture, offering a transformative space for personal growth and spiritual exploration.

The innovator of the Spiritually Fly™ philosophy, Faith has transcended traditional boundaries to establish it as a holistic lifestyle brand for wellness and personal transformation. Originally conceived as a dynamic fusion of breathwork, movement, sound, and stillness — quintessentially tailored for the modern era yet firmly anchored in yogic tradition — Spiritually Fly™ has blossomed into a comprehensive wellness lifestyle brand. This revolutionary approach initially centered around traditional yogic methods, has evolved significantly under Faith's guidance.

Drawing upon her extensive knowledge, spiritual and academic studies, prolific writing skills, and rich real-life experiences, Faith has expanded Spiritually Fly™ beyond its original framework. Today, it encompasses a broad spectrum of modalities, including the insights of Kundalini and Hatha yoga, various meditation techniques, and ancient teachings. These elements collectively work to elevate the body, mind, and soul. Faith's teachings imbued with vitality and contemporary relevance, artfully weave spiritual practices into the tapestry of modern-day experiences. This unique blend helps people maintain a grounded connection to their soul and captures the radiant essence and expansive nature of the Spiritually Fly lifestyle.

As an author and creative soul, Faith has seamlessly merged her passion for poetry into her spiritual practice. Her first work, 'Shades of the Soul: A Meditation Journal,' is a testament to this fusion, offering a mix of original poetry and daily inspirations. Her authorial prowess extends to the acclaimed and celebrated 'Spiritually Fly: Wisdom, Meditations, and Yoga to Elevate Your Soul,' a beacon of guidance for those seeking a deeper connection with their spiritual essence.

Faith is a sought-after figure at major wellness events, from the Great Lawn of Central Park to international stages like Wanderlust 108, enchanting attendees with her unique blend of meditation and yoga. Her expertise has earned her a spot on the esteemed faculty at Kripalu, Yogaville, Omega, and the Art of Living. Featured on prestigious platforms like Yoga Journal, Om Yoga & Lifestyle, ORIGIN, and Sweat Equity, her influence extends beyond the mat. Appearances in Essence, Black Enterprise, Women's Health, Shape, and more, further amplify her reach. A key instructor for Beachbody's three-week yoga retreat, Faith also shares her insights on platforms like iFit/NordicTrack, Fitbit, Gaia, OmStars, DoYouYoga, Alo Moves, and TINT Yoga. Her role as a wellness philanthropist, movement motivator, healing guide, and Spiritually Fly theorist is complemented by her love for music and her cherished fur baby, Sebastian.

Faith Hunter is not just a meditation and yoga instructor; she's a guiding light in the journey towards wellness, embodying the essence of a Spiritually Fly life.

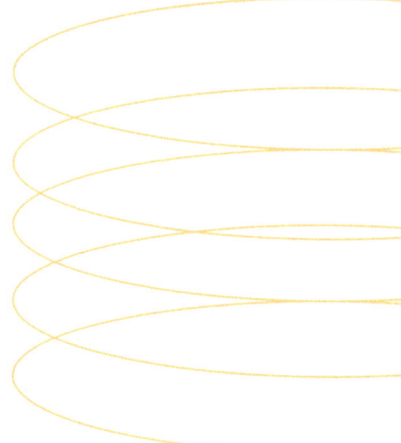

free yourself from the restrictions of fear
expand into the greatness of your beauty
raise the vibration of your spirit
live the life you see in your dreams
dance fiercely in the rivers of divinity
listen to your intuition and be guided by
your heart

www.ingramcontent.com/pod-product-compliance
Lightning Source LLC
Chambersburg PA
CBHW070716130626
46553CB00005B/2011